Double Edge
Kay Syrad

Double Edge
© Kay Syrad and Pighog Press 2012

Design by curiouslondon.com

Kay Syrad has asserted her right to be identified as the author of this work in accordance with the Copyright, Designs and Patents Act 1998.

All rights reserved. No part of this pamphlet may be reproduced, stored in a retrieval system, or transmitted in any form, or by any means, electronic or otherwise, without the prior written permission of Pighog Press.

ISBN 978-1-906309-23-7

First published May 2012 by

Pighog Press

PO Box 145
Brighton BN1 6YU
England UK

info@pighog.co.uk
www.pighog.co.uk
www.facebook.com/Pighog
www.twitter.com/Pighog

The Doves in the Green Leaves

The white doves floated
in the green leaves

and the boys' shouting
flew about the girls,

their arms stretched out
on the ground behind—

and beyond her wood bench
a nut of colour plumed,

scarlet red, singly.
She strained for words

to carry back
her gratefulness, but

the sky caught her,
the land stilled her.

The Taxonomer's Girl

I dropped my fresh free posy. It flared,
flew and lay down quiet on the dark
oak floor. The stems listed, the petals
floated, curious in their new night sky.

I knelt down over my fresh free posy,
brought the tip of my finger to meet
the lapped pink petals, dared to frisk
the lustred filaments, fearless as day.

I heard his dry and even tread, gathered
up the fresh and fallen posy, my palm
tender from its thorns. Sweet wild rose,
Sir, I whispered: see its rounded leaves.

He held my wrist, led me to his sunlit desk,
bade me give up my flowers to his lexicon.

Archive

The other thing was that I'd been in the library
all afternoon, resting my eyes on the words
'cathedral mauve' and 'rose damask',
thinking how light moves through a church
from east to west, silver at noon, gold at five;

resting my eyes on the small black letters
set deep in thin paper, and the archive box itself:
thick buff pulp, reinforced corners. The delicate
papers lay flat inside a blue folder, with samples
of fabric placed calmly at the top, without pins -

placed there by a man in 1924—Perkins, a man
so pure and sweetly serious, so skilled and knowing,
that my pleasure in reading about dyes and silks,
cottons and serge was such that I would rather
read about them for ever than look at them directly.

Owl with Blue Pencil

We met at the Romanesque entrance,
I admired your hair in its quiff,
the wool skirt outlining your hips,
your black pointed boots –
and then our arms and hands
were all about each other:
we were in from the cold,
sipping coffee, milk on our lips,
a little nervous, positioning,
until we went out among the cabinets -
saw humming birds small
as your thumb, the furred knees
of a song thrush, a tailor-bird's nest
stitched to leaves; birds dissected,
feathers combed and named,
quill ends dipped in red dye;
and - next to the crowned pigeon
with its delicate fan of feathers on stems,
above the single, floating feather
of a nestling albatross –
the severed head of an owl
with a thick, blue pencil
pushed horizontally
into one of its ornamental 'ears'.

In the next room, we stroked
the glass over two famous finches
on faux-velvet, admired
a pillow-frog's breathing,
tried to decipher notes
in the red book marked E.
Later, we sipped plum vodka
and borscht; we were warm,
our faces dipped and rose,
our gestures mimetic; our voices,
piping and cooing, were finely tuned –
until we marched out into the freezing wind,
our words flying up among the trees.
We said goodbye on the double-decker -
I watched you descend the subway,
a flurry of snow in your hair -
and the birds sang on in our minds.

For Jane Wildgoose

Lefebvre's Objects

Objects touch one another. Feel, smell and hear
   one another. Gloriously.

And objects, newly-sentient, gilt-mirrored or lit ruby,
   veiled, electrified
or shrivel-shrunk by reckless placing—
(blush of tin with jewels on velvet,
   burly-hewn stone in hand-sewn silk—)

objects held once by the limits of perception—
      are here flung free
in bronze-beating, stair-swelling, realm-bursting joy.

The Soane Museum

Light was brought in by colour: Pompei-red walls in the drawing room, the yellow morning room with yellow drapes, the oil-green walls of the oval atrium, the brass frame over the sarcophagus. Light was concealed, too, behind the panelled doors that opened to reveal the Bank of England drawings *(designs for the Debt Redemption Offices)* and the Hogarths - and in Napoleon's ring of hair.

And your room, with the storm lanterns that night, flame light reflected in the table and in strips of mirror either side of the bookcase, catching a fragment of two spotted china cups, whitening the two mole skeletons, remarking on two tiny blue eggs. Light on pairs that mirrored our friendship: back to back; the same or similar; on the plaster insect moulds repeated in the mirrored table - and in the sheen of the Linnaeus cabinets, with two bottom drawers open for an explanation.

The Convalescents
September 1876

I came down on the London train
with the two sweet Sisters and Milly,
got hoisted into a cart at Eastbourne
and followed the slow sea road to the Home.
I breathed in the great sea beast,
letting it swirl round my lungs
and I sat close to Milly as she swished her hair,
her mouth wide as ribbons
and the Sisters smirked, their eyes
loose silver in the bright sea sun.
Then we were turning away, facing
white hills above a high flint wall,
the stone march of windows
over orange brick, and chimneys,
and Milly *I love her* was standing with Sister
and their suitcases at what they called
the 'women's entrance', a pointed arch
of darkness with the curves of a whalebone
or a ship's hull, or a woman.
I clutched the collars of my coat as the driver
swung us away and out to sea again.
The Sister touched my arm, flicked
her eyes towards the north gate
and through we went to the men's entrance,
a dark mirror to the women's.
I was entering a foreign place.

I ducked my head and narrowed my eyes
so recently wide with the racing sea.
Inside I saw Milly on the stairway, rising,
a column of light on her hair.
I stepped forward on the polished stones,
traced the curve of the balustrade
until I could hold no more light in my eyes.
The sound was seagulls, near and far,
their beaks pointed arches in the sky
and my chest ached, my blood felt thin.
Milly, I called up, *Milly* and was shushed
by Sister and taken to my Ward.
There I contemplated Heaven,
the carving of the stone, the floor
a white lake. I put my hands together,
knelt my knees on a bony floor -
cried with the effort and the pain.
Thirteen other beds, a man coughing
Got a smoke, lad? and Sister, finger
to lip, pointing at *The Rules*.
Dreamed and dreamed of Milly in the night:
she held black railings above her head,
she held wild sea waves in her hair,
a bird swam by with arms and legs.
Milly sang, and after placed her lips on mine,
lips red as muscle, and I was shouting
'Oh! Oh—!' until a stinging burnt my cheek
and Sister's candle lit her marble eye.

And so I slept again, went in and out
of men's and women's rooms,
up our separate stairs,
saw women weaving thorns
around the silvered floors.
Next morning the lads and I faced out to sea,
a plain and shivered row.
We pulled our blankets to our chins
and groaned, and groaned again,
our faces stretched in wind,
a spit of rain cast down to help us live.
Below, the greening sea and creamy sand,
behind, the deer flank hills,
and beside us, the nurses' blue skirts beat
against a sky the milky grey
of Milly's eyes. And inside my chest,
a lone saw rocked back and forth through bone,
and pain became a reach—
a skill one learnt by stealth.

Subverting the Order of Things

This is an entry from the Yale catalogue of Entomology:
"a prodigious wasp's nest: *genus* Hymenoptera: *species*
Vespidae: Dolichovespula Maculata". A hornet, its face
bald, long antennae, forewings and hindwings on a body

dressed in black leather with white epaulettes and a striped
white tail. It's the females who sport the ovipositors
and the power to sting; and they all have tongues or glossas,
a proboscis with labia palpus, in a bright shocking red.

But I know a collector who refuses to provide any details
of provenance, preferring to allow the object, the specimen
simply to thrill and resonate, evoke memory and association,

fall out of the nested hierarchy, the shallow mahogany
drawer, into a luscious heterarchy of amethyst, ginger
and water-lilies, with their horizontal perspectives on authority.

Cicada

On our second day we found
the first dry ghosts
stuck to the trunk of a tree
as if edging forward, the size
of a girl's thumb, hollow,
backs cracked open.
The empty, fibrous casings
were the colour of dust
or the shallow basins
of the ancient wash-house
by the side of the road.

Then we saw her,
at the base of a branch,
still sewn to her shadow:
pale lime, wings silver-white
spotted with lemon or gold
and folded along the length
of her narrow, wet pulsing body.
Caught as if dressing –
tender, and elegant.
We looked away, unnerved.

In the full heat of noon
we cycled home, crush
 of their sound in our ears:
the breathy sawing
of the male cicadas -
their two ribbed membranes
contracting and buckling
in the abdominal chamber -
each call scaling,
echoing the last call.

Yet they say the cicada
lives on dew and air,
nothing inside but eloquence,
the fifth string of the Greek cithara,
or our own winged souls.

Anni des Cevennes

Each year, on her birthday,
her son sends a small box. Inside,
a red maple leaf from Connecticut,
perhaps a diamanté brooch
he found on a path, or the satin
bow from a starlet's shoe.

She eases up the lid, hears it sigh.
Lipstick – she twists up scarlet,
slides it across her lower lip,
side to side. Two mother-of-pearl
buttons taped to a piece of card,
a square of blood red silk -
she'll sew it into her coat,
see it flash as she gathers
the coat around her.

Outside, the trees march
up and down, amber, resin;
sheep and goats graze
on the sheer slope.
Her son used to hide out
in the chesnut houses, come
home late with his pockets full.
Show me, she'd cry, *let me see!*

Your father will come, she says.
He does not come.

Once, he drives his brown van
into the village. The boy runs
from side to side of the road,
the chickens scatter, the dog barks.
The van stops and the son climbs up
to sit alongside his father.
The two face forward, silent.
The father's forearms are strong,
a black moustache sweeps his lip.
The boy sees straw and ropes
in the back, a rifle.

Anni stands at the kitchen door,
her mouth a square;
she holds a goose in her arms,
wrapped in a cloth.
The father grips the steering wheel
and sighs. The boy stares.
Maman, he says.
The father climbs out of the van.
He gives the mother fifty, a hundred,
she folds the notes with the hand
not holding the goose.
Her mouth is closed.

The father calls, *descend-toi!*
The van reverses, sucks up gravel
between the sandstone house
and the hay barn,
rolls past the big walnut tree,
past the sheep,
round the hairpin bend,
down and smaller, the boy
running down the bank,
stopping for breath on the low path.
Papa.

Anni des Cevennes sits
with a wood bowl on her knees
cracking walnuts in a vice.
Why is he my father?
She looks up at the boy.
He is a good man, she says.
Why doesn't he live here?
Anni takes up another nut,
settles it into place.
Maman.
He goes outside to re-enact
the moment of his father arriving,
to make his father appear
and disappear in the Citroën van,
make Maman appear
with the wrapped goose.

Outside, the trees march up
and down, the sheep and goats
graze on the sheer slope.
The son does not visit,
instead he sends things
he has held in his palm:
a pearl button, a feather -
and Anni des Cevennes,
wings opening and closing,
feeds the cats in the yard,
takes her favourites
to bed at night,
lets them claw lightly
at her hair.

Allihies

West coast of Ireland: all rock erosion and silk water,
  windows shrouded in fuschia, roads defined by pubs:
O'Sullivan's, Lighthouse Bar, Oak, O'Neill's Bar,
  and the houses line up turquoise, scarlet, green daub.

Patrick Silver's selling crabs-claws, mackerel, pollack
  from the boot of his car and the boats are bringing
the evening light across the bay. She's walking back
  over the bog, falling down, gathering up wet, stumbling

towards the Minane Cliffs, dragging up to the limit
  of the cliffs, past the broken cairn that marks the night,
towards the black rocks—the beautiful rocks, her heart

  advancing, mind riding with the boats in the last light,
and in Oak Bar a man is singing, low and unaccompanied,
  while she's falling down long, black and long to the sea.

"Registering their flora,/their fauna"

The fog-harvesting beetle has smooth, peaked surfaces
    with troughs of water-repelling wax –
it tilts its back and water-droplets roll into its mouth;

the larvae of the stag beetle live inside dead oak for five years;
    in the iridescent blue beetle the scales are stacked,
layer upon layer, light accumulating;

only in polarised moonlight can the dung beetle
    roll its ball in a straight line;
and the water-beetle carries fish eggs on its fins:

and so she makes you wait,
    her colours placed, geometry in the fold-up
chairs in lantern light - *two different lanterns,* the lights

swinging, and there - *the rose red rock roses;*
    listening, and waiting, not even waiting – until all
the winged Madeira beetles have been blown out to sea.

Burnt Island Lake

When he heard the pure, long calling of the loon,
  a strong swooping majestic call, early,
when the loon had dominion over the black lake,
  only the loon and its echo beyond Tree Island,
he tried to place it with another sound:
  Régine Crespin singing Berlioz, perhaps;
and when the loon called once more,
  three muscled, rolling syllables, he thought:

one of Charcot's hysterics in a high French room.
  Yesterday, at Alder Lake, he'd been trapped
in a gold swamp by beavers' dams
  and he'd cursed the beaver as it swam towards its lodge
for he'd hoped to see a moose in the forest,
  to match its big round paw prints
with the shadow-prints of the water boatmen
  curiously enlarged as the sun met the water's surface—

instead he paddled back to the rock-and-sand
  promontory where he slept in a tent with his wife.
'Try just listening,' his wife had said,
  touching his mouth with her fingers,
and they'd listened to the whirr of a humming bird,
  two red squirrels chasing each other
in the pine trees, water against rock, flies,
  and the wind in its private rushing.

He was bored with listening.
  He read his book, just his sort of book:
a European journey, both acerbic and romantic,
  and he sat with his back straight
against a tree in Algonquin reading about Poland,
  New York and Vancouver, the 60s, 70s,
the years when he too began to place things,
  when he began to rejoice in equivalence.

But his wife had thrown off her clothes,
  her limbs had turned golden under small waves
and the sunlight was making her glitter.
  He wanted to follow her, wanted to be
that glittering figure in the water.
  He edged forward, like the little hornet
with its sticky pads—but already his wife
  was dry, throwing trail mix to a chipmunk,

gathering wood for a fire. He retrieved his book
  and flicked through the pages,
reading about exile, thinking about symmetry
  (and the two fine lake bream he'd caught
for their supper). Then he could hear the loon calling
  again and he closed his eyes: a series of long,
echoing loops, the echo of the loon bringing
  the lake inward, calling the lake to heel.

Snow Curtain

Soon, the snow will fall in through the window.
I am blind. The snow, the blue: they are my eyes.

The fall—the snow falling in through the window,
the window that sees, sees me. A small horizon

forms in the curtain itself: zigzags and diamonds
floating, like the snow curtain, floating in the blue

room (dark bed, blue cloth). I have no understanding,
faced with a whiteness that listens, waits, sees,

presses in, for the snow is pressing in at the curtain.
Yet its parts, particles, they cannot make whole, and

I can feel the snow pressing in, a square of imposition
against my black edge, here where white, blue, hurt me.

Blue Bench

I looked and looked again at the blue bench,
blue—not flame-blue or vapour-blue, nor that

blue of ice beneath its surface, but oil-blue,
plastic. It faced, double, symmetrical, towards

and away from sea and land. I sat and looked away,
screed of sea behind, my feet in the choppy sand.

I caught a glimpse of certainty, but not the tide
draping itself about my legs—and I turned

to face out the full, light, breasting beam
of the horizon. Only when I was drowned—

my mind filled up with simple waves—could I
know the limit of a back-to-back slatted bench,

the circle of outward and inward gaze meeting,
and begin to place my heart upright, vertical.

Double Edge
for Thomas Joshua Cooper

I

Norway. Europe - its north-most northern point
in the Barents Sea: this is where light leaks
from the photographer's hands like milk and streaks
the black rock promiscuously; or moves to anoint

the sandstone crag, as the dark slopes in front
call up the angel, the net of spray that speaks
each time the sea swells, each time it breaks,
makes powdered bone and zinc for silverpoint.

And here, he deepens the black and so the density
of the light; light makes the edge, the line.
Yet it's not the line itself that gives us possibility,

but where the line is interrupted, veiled by fine
mist. And between black time and white eternity
he leaves us, at our north-most north imagining.

II

He leaves us at our north-most north imagining,
sails where currents pluck blistered wrack
through the Pillars of Hercules, where ships crack
and fling their silk on rock, where the sea sings

with Atlantic memory. Hear low whispering
as the wind whips waves into ribs, cloaks
muscled figures of the classical world, sucks
fish to the surface, throws them back as coins.

Here he shepherds the waves, makes light descend
in bones of rain, breaks a white wave on the fan
of a dark wave roaring free, lets souls ascend.

And now he spreads a shadow where the world ends
so we cannot know where God turns back and Man
begins, only borders the photographer intends.

III

Begins, ends, borders the photographer intends
for Africa, Cape Verde where the sea cries
in syncopated rhythm, where the sea sighs
and hisses 'what is— what is the sea' but veins

and wraiths and vortices? Here feel the dense
suck of a wave that curls and tucks, rises
and breathes, its arc muscular and fresh and high.
Watch its luminous haul lease height and length

to foam. He nearly died for this, stretched low
counting waves from low tide to high tide, his eye
abandoned to gold, to the promise of tone.

Awoke in hospital: tripod, camera by his pillow
lens, black hoods, all exact, and knowing why
time itself gives east and west, above, below.

IV

Time itself gives east and west, above, below:
see Cap Manuel, basalt, schist, in Dakar night
where rock is charged, hand-placed by light
each edge distinct, its surface hallowed.

And beyond the lit rock, a soundless mellow
sea where a single wave cast faintly left to right
divides the picture. The line creates angle, invites
measure: geometry on geology. A double arrow

carved white in black rock excites the reach—
Africa to America—human crossing, touch point.
Here we apprehend the language of *extreme,*

extremity, furthest from centre, to follow the sea's
milk thread, know the meaning of *front
line*: a breath begun at dawn in east-most east.

V

Line: the breath begun at dawn in east-most east
now declares immanence in merciless spray
that foams and flies through soaked rock drapes,
fires and dies at sea-snakes' throats, that feasts

itself on light. This is Robben Island, its coast
facing out to Cape Town on Freedom Day,
the photographer waiting in as the sea flays
all thought from mind, strips it of its violence.

The spray falls abstract into an inner frame,
and here he renders mass, allows light to speak
yet holds the light between lit fingers,

holds in tension dark and light, wild, tame,
to touch below the surface, beyond technique.
Even in the formless white, form lingers.

VI

Even in the formless white, form lingers.
In straws of silver rain; in time dropped frozen
from a moon-stained sky on the west Norwegian
Sea, where light fillets the waves and mirrored

air is a dress—lit clouds dress the water.
A white ball flashes and rises behind the rain
and floats, all surface, forsaking horizon:
light answering dark as the sea aligns its feathers.

Here he defies land: there is only sea and man,
and life in lengths he chooses. Here is Wilde's
optimism over experience, hope flung open,

concept sacrificed to lust: pure, raw, found
in the double image, the moon and its bride.
This, the photographer's point of no return.

VII

And this, the photographer's point of no return:
at the mouths of four rivers, at first light
or last, light buried beneath the water's sight
and named 'very light grey, grey', texture

a mask; and 'silver, very dark grey—almost
black.' The task, one single exposure, tide
measured, shadows suspended, pattern denied.
Comet Trail, Madeira; Bay of Biscay: never

chanced, each frame a double edge: end, start,
the sea's skim from Old World to mewling
New, only compass laying north and south apart—

and 'The sky very slightly burned in.' A chart
of the sea's inhuman gift of nothing or everything,
a record of a wave rising, falling, in a human heart.

Lidl Bag

A wild bush, a wreck in the prairie,
roots strewn like raked hair, or rope;

a red plastic can (unknown) (mute), and
the white Lidl bag with its yellow sun;

white stones on sand, hard and dry;
a layered sky with flying grey clouds

beneath puff white; light refracting
on red hidden in the bush; the shimmer

of reeds, line of light cutting behind
(is it an island?)—and she exploits colour

while I remember my thirst for a pure,
absolute red, my fear when I find it –

its prismatic origin, the way it harbours,
ingests, breaks all known colours.

Floating Yellow Sauna

You're naked and the ground isn't even
steady beneath you; you're floating naked

in a hay-bale sauna with a circus roof
and red log ballast; you're naked among

the bright green reeds, with the sun on
your circus hat, with a bright red ballast

log behind you; you're alive on the blue
water in the green reeds in the yellow sun

of the evening; you are hot cold hot cold
hot cold and steam fills your eyes, steams

you, drips you, dips you; you leave steam
for cool water, dash the cool blue water,

spoil the smooth, cool water round the screen
of reeds, green reeds, the tall green reeds.

Yellow Hut

A bank of dunes under a black sky, a tormented
sky barely able to hold its weather—will it

loose its boiling clouds? —and uncertain footprints
pit the sand (alongside, stopped). Here the horizon

line is sucked towards the yellow hut, the sky,
racing, is sucked towards the yellow hut, and clouds

are flattened out. To the right of the hut, sand
morphs into sea, only an intermittent petticoat

of surf dividing the two; and the wind arranges itself
into an amphitheatre of sand, palely tossed about

the yellow hut. Sweep of cloud, sweep of sand
and light, all the time, the yellow, yellow hut,

between land and sky, windowless, and doorless,
excites us to its essence: colour its only function.

Inside the Hut

There is a hut, it has no door. It cannot be penetrated.
There is a hut: colour, light—the hut is a colour,

it sits on the horizon, alone. It is my mother.
My mother is the hut, with a little colour;

she is there in the light. (I was ready to love.
I will love, in time). My mother is there in the light,

let my mother be there in the light. Let my, let my,
let my mother, my mother—I am inside the hut:

here it is dark. All I have is mouth. The hut is long
and dark. The horizon speaks. The wind brings

light, my mother speaks – ah, ah – I am listening,
I am tense with listening. I listen. I call to the dark.

Tatiana's Visit

Outside, behind the leaves, the hill is a strip
of white sand. Inside, I raise my knuckles,
bring them to the wall—You hear me at once,
far away: you are far away when you hear.

I bring the wall towards you, bring the air
to you, gathered in my fist. Behind the wall
you eat bread, soup, black grapes (you tear
one from its stem—let your lips close).

*The window's a bocca di lupo, with bars
on the inside; all I can see is a stretch of sky—
(Tania, Julca—please, tell my boys to write.)*

Outside, on the white sand, I pray for you,
and you don't pray—ever—each of us standing
on our high, stony ground, our hearts starving.

Bunker

Above the horizon, blue, indigo:
principle of dark. Below,

a concrete hut with a slot-mouth
lists in a river of stones.

At the slot's lip, a white stain
(paint or chalk) draws the eye to

lichen. The drift and spread
of stones around the hut suggests

bluff, a reckless casting, while
a felted black in the foreground

cries out for *end*, the *gone* of it, cries
out to the black-hatted priest beyond.

The Gallerist

We are on the slope, our mouths
wanton from the mackerel and
hard-boiled eggs. The men bring
Anya along the path. No, she brings
the men along the path. We look
towards her, the woman who brings
our men along the path, a woman
with high apricot stretched over her
lips. The men gesture towards us.
She stands still whilst the men own
us, we have time to examine her filmy
eyes, the black headband with white
polka dots over henna'd grey hair. 'And
this is *my* wife.' My eyes, for the briefest
longest second, are able to rest in hers.

We follow Anya to the white barn.
Inside, we face six granite monoliths
placed round a square. We feel awe
and we feel cold. Anya stands with
her back to the wall and talks. We listen,
each in turn daring to edge away to
study the granite blocks, aware of
the scrape of our boots. The light
in the barn meets the mica in the stone;
the girders are red, the roof grey.
'Yes, it is cold', says Anya. 'The artist
says to me, as he gets older he gets more
cold. He wishes this to be represented
in his work.' We think of his old bones
cold beneath his skin, how a heart ices over.

We stare at Anya's olive jeans and
listen to names: Long, Lang, Nash,
Leib, Zurich, Woodstock. We let
our eyes draw up the granite columns
once more and file out of the white
barn. Anya is tall amongst us as we
move towards the artist's cottage,
see his paintings on the walls. 'Bauhaus,'
she says. 'All the furniture, Bauhaus.'
In the courtyard a man and a boy
load a grand piano into a horse-box.
The man speaks to Anya in a high
aristocratic moan, we cannot tell
what he says. We walk a high tunnel
of rusting trees, see the empty lake.

Anya brings us along the path to her
house, makes coffee, puts out a single
pastry. We sit at her ash table, our eyes
sneak over the walls, the books. With
the dark coffee on our lips we see
the photograph, a dead person,
blood on his arm and his neck, grainy.
'It is the first photographic still from
television to become art,' she says.
We are impressed and dismayed. We
have brought in our mackerel and eggs
and the men eat. Anya picks at her single
pastry. 'The artist is in Germany,' she
says. 'He was homesick for his language.'
We think she was the artist's lover.

The tall elegant Anya with high apricot
lips. She is seventy, her eyes are pale,
she is sixty five, her eyes are mischievous.
She shows pictures of her Hamburg
Gallery, 1970s: Anya's long legs and
delicate lips, Anya with the artists,
Hockney, Warhol. One by one we creep
up the narrow stairs to her bathroom,
our eye caught first by a poster of
Tracy Emin in the bath, her dark nipples
floating on the paper's surface, then
by a Mapplethorpe: glistening hips,
a graceful penis. On her shelves, five
wristwatches, a dozen perfumes,
the John Lennon and Yoko Ono bag.

'Yes, he is homesick, he is tired.' And
cold, we remember, too cold to keep
on loving Anya. 'But tomorrow I go
to the Hunt Ball! I take my tartan
bedspread, drape it round my body,
on top my black jacket and no-one
suspects a thing. When first I was in
London I wore my green velvet
curtains to every party. Tomorrow
I am Ambassador's guest, he is gay,
everyone knows it, but always he takes
a woman to the Ball.' I imagine the two
at the Hunt Ball, the Ambassador as
the woman, Anya his male escort, the
Ambassador hung with tartan, green velvet.

Joan

I took my friend to the bluebell woods. She walked very slowly, past the low ferns, and the white wood anemones, and amongst the bluebells. We went further in. She saw moss at the root of a tree. She leant forward and smoothed the moss with her left hand, first with her palm, and then with the backs of her fingers.

For Maurice

I

I was shocked by your yellow skin,
how slight you'd become.
I pressed your fingers to my face.
We talked and cried, let the crying
drain the serif from our words -
words now unforming and gathering
behind bone at a place
only light, or birds, may describe.

II

I was in France when you died,
climbing ancient steps, gazing down
on hot grids of vines and cypress.

Back home, I'm sure we saw you -
in boughs of yellow-pink plums,
among the red-spotted Burnet moths.
We saw you, didn't we,
by the lagoon at Cuckmere,
in the blue gorse?
It was you, surely, that fox cub
who stopped by the barn,
slowly turned his eyes towards us
and sauntered away,
his tail filleted by the rapping wind.

Loss

Does it tilt, or list
in its chamber?

What is its drop?

(Her hair is long—
the frayed ends
of her heart).

What is its span?

(Call the line gentle
as roses.)

What sound
does the heart make
in the felled air?

(There are small scars
on her fingers).

Ride

from a window table in the bristol arms
I can see the rides on brighton pier
the arm of a crane that lifts a chair slow
high   and higher waits *let her not be harmed*
swoops wide out over a grey-black sea

the afternoon sun (it's spring) is low
she fell so low and kate bush sings
her wuthering heights   her voice strung
thin and strange   *let her not be harmed*

in the swell of sound the big wheel
turns   the chair is rising and below the joggers
on the promenade are toned and strong
let her be strong and the arm of the crane
lifts for its long descent   *my sweet love*

**I remember leaving,
being left**

I was taken in a car in the arms of a nurse,
on the back seat, it was a black Ford Popular,
the seats were red leather, the dashboard
red metal - this is what the nurse saw -
and my face was against her wool cape,
before I knew wool or nurses, only
shape or dark or light. I remember leaving
my mother – taken away, whisked, snatched,
ferreted - and the noise: hollow of tin,
squeaking lino, a loud slapping. I remember
leaving my mother, sailing away, flying
through the air, through the fresh breeze
of my mother's hair, far now from the milky
warmth, her cardigan. I wanted to stay,
circle, hover above – and it's as if I died in the air –
and came back to life at the level of feet,
white shoes, black shoes turning – *bring her
this way* - and the babies were crying
high and wide, near me.

Sarcophagus

She is hung, or placed, rich,
all her lives within: a mass
of jewels and twine, some
trailing provocatively,
endlessly—

Hung above,
on a receding wall, or placed -
find her dark at your feet.
Inside the sac, colour: lapis,
gold, bright ruby.
It is where she rests, without
weight or temperature,
and where she dreams
(orange groves, water).

The sac remains unmarked
by light for years;
hangs like hock
while men speak to
an empty room, or touch:
watch her slow spin
on unwound thread—

Slow spin, until the grown
body slips to the floor,
unfettered,
and the air is surprising.
Here is an other-where:
she crawls, slithers, finds length.

Clear Structure

The structure is wide, it goes off the frame, appears
to have no end or purpose. It is given by the light

and seized by the light, reveals only a burnished half.
It is open to the white sky's rushing: angles and grid-

lines turning black or silvering. Its horizontal lines
meet the horizon; its verticality is human—and it pulls

away, pulls us away by its incompleteness, becomes
a vessel we must fill. That wood floor, measured

lengths planed and fitted, surely a floor for dancing.
(The band plays, the musicians all women, their men

dead; the movement of their bodies slow, unified.
At home the grates are unswept, the bread coarse.

The women's eyes are small. The dancing helps
them live - in the burnished, radiant half they live.)

Letter from my Brother

When I saw those words a goose flew into my chest
and beat its wings in there, and there was laughing

on the other side, where all the chickens, the litters,
were scrambling up the sides and down, on the grass,

falling over each other in their innocence. Fresh-daisy
excitement! The sun beating down on our heads,

the laughing, the beach huts, the long promenade
with the huge round pebbles below, the wind, the light-

grey of the sea wall and the suck of that wind, pulling
our faces into smiles, smiling itself; the stripes, awning,

rain – and always the laughter, incessant, long—ours.
Our show, our imagined world, the singing, chancing,

and everywhere the awning. We were stiff as frost,
folded, stacked, but the breath on the glass was ours.

Carnival of the Lazy Kings

I see him slow, in orange light, in smoke,
his long black hair sleek and black, see him mourn
the golden float, the lazy klezmer slow
and low, low and slack. And the red plush Kings
are riding high, their golden thrones high and light
as the song unfurls in the feathered black.

Two pierrots propel the float, white and black
on one-wheeled bikes, pull the float long and slow
- a giant's bed with wrought-iron sides. The Kings
swing from a treble clef in golden light -
sway through a tall, a hungry arch, pink smoke
pink on poplar leaves. And I watch him mourn

a love; I love his love, blue-black, I mourn
his love (this orange glow, the klezmer slow
and lazy, slow and long, the arches black,
the pierrots flying white and high, the smoke
in the leaves, in the poplar trees, the Kings
in plush, in red plush thrones in blazing light).

We move slow and crimson, slow in the light,
following the floats and the rococo Kings
who sing like fish to the silver night. Black
are his shoulders and his long smooth hair, slow
his step, his graceful step, and what I mourn
is love's plush rising in the slow red smoke.

The pierrots gesture in red, through smoke
at a gold wire bird circling in the black,
high as the poplars, high above the Kings,
those louche and Lazy Kings - and I mourn
my love, his silk black hair sleek in the light,
his step, his lost love floating in the slow

red rising of the night. His love is slow,
it circles long, I long for love, I mourn
the silver dark. The floats are still, the light
above is dazzling bright, my heart is black
and a gold wire bird turns slow in the smoke,
the orange-pink smoke of the Lazy Kings.

I mourn him, long and slow in orange light,
in the flare smoke pink of the Lazy Kings,
mourn his love, long, sleek and tulip black.

Casa de la Memoria

on the wooden boards
the singer calls

the dancer is ready
smooth as ink

the heels of their hands
will cup together

like wood
cup cup

and she is on the boards
in her tiered skirts

arms high
fingers are bones

snapping
her feet rocking

the cup cup of the men
their muted voices

cup cup of the wood
the murmurs of the men

black shoes
on the wood

cup cupping
the men are cup cupping

and her fingers speak
her fingers speak

her fingers speak
her fingers her fingers

cup cup
cup cupping

he has untied his hair
loosened his silk

he is ready on the boards
his shirt red

trousers black
shoes

black
heels ready

and she
is cup cupping her hands

she is ready
the singer is ready

the guitar is ready
ay! cup cupping

she looks at him
her eyelashes

he is on the boards
his fingers mute

lips moving
heels snapping

neat   compact
heels snapping

on the boards
he is wet

his shirt red
he snaps with his hips

her shoes on the boards
on the boards

a thunder on the boards
shoes rocking
one one one one
fast fast

shoes heels
black speed of the rocking

her legs
long in their stockings

his head is tipped
and she murmurs

she murmurs
cup cupping her hands

she murmurs
cup cupping her hands

she murmurs
she murmurs

cup cupping

Notes

In 'Lefebvre's Objects', the phrases 'Objects touch one another. Feel, smell and hear/ one another' are taken from Henri Lefebvre's *The Production of Space*.

The title 'Registering their flora/their fauna' is taken from Elizabeth Bishop's poem, 'Crusoe in England'.

'Double Edge' was written in response to Thomas Joshua Cooper's exhibition of photographs, Point of No Return.

In 'Tatiana's Visit', the italicised lines are from Antonio Gramsci's prison letters, slightly adapted. Gramsci, philosopher and founder of the Italian Communist Party, was imprisoned for many years under Mussolini's regime. His wife Julia ('Julca') moved back to Russia with their two sons, but her sister, Tatiana, who was a devout Catholic, visited him regularly in prison.

Acknowledgements are due to the editors of the following publications in which these poems (or similar versions of them) have appeared:

'Registering their flora/their fauna' was published in Poetry Review and later Artemis. 'Allihies', 'Tatiana's Visit' and 'Loss' were published in Envoi, 'Joan' was published in Smiths Knoll. 'The Convalescents' appeared in Long Poem Magazine, 'Archive', 'Double Edge', 'The Gallerist' and 'Carnival of the Lazy Kings' appeared in the Enitharmon Press anthology I am Twenty People, and 'Archive' also in Poetry South East 2010.

The Templar Competition anthologies Buzz and Stripe included, respectively, 'Letter to my Brother' and 'Burnt Island Lake'. 'Lidl Bag', 'Yellow Hut', 'Inside the Hut', 'Floating Yellow Sauna', 'Bunker', 'Snow Curtain', 'Clear 'Structure' and 'Blue Bench' first appeared in Objects of Colour: Baltic Coast (Foxhall Publishing) and 'Double Edge' was also printed in a small hand-sewn edition of 50 by East Port Editions.

'The Taxonomer's Girl' was commissioned by Rother District Council and appeared with artworks inside buses travelling between Hastings and Rother. A version of 'For Maurice' was published on the website www.likestarlings.com.

I would also like to thank all the people who have generously supported and advised me in the writing of these poems.